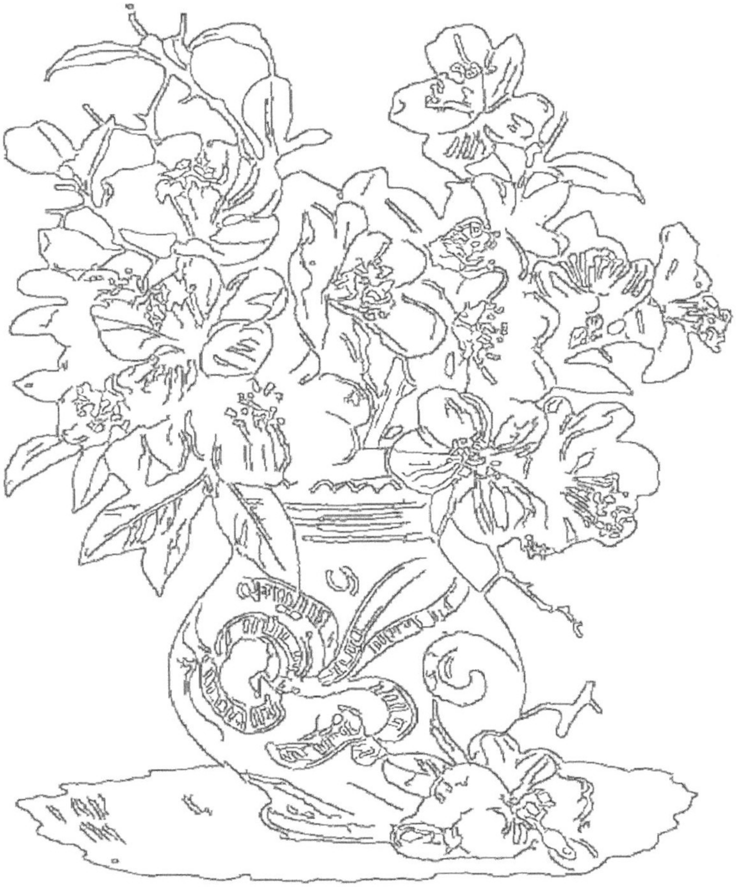

Enjoy Coloring !!!

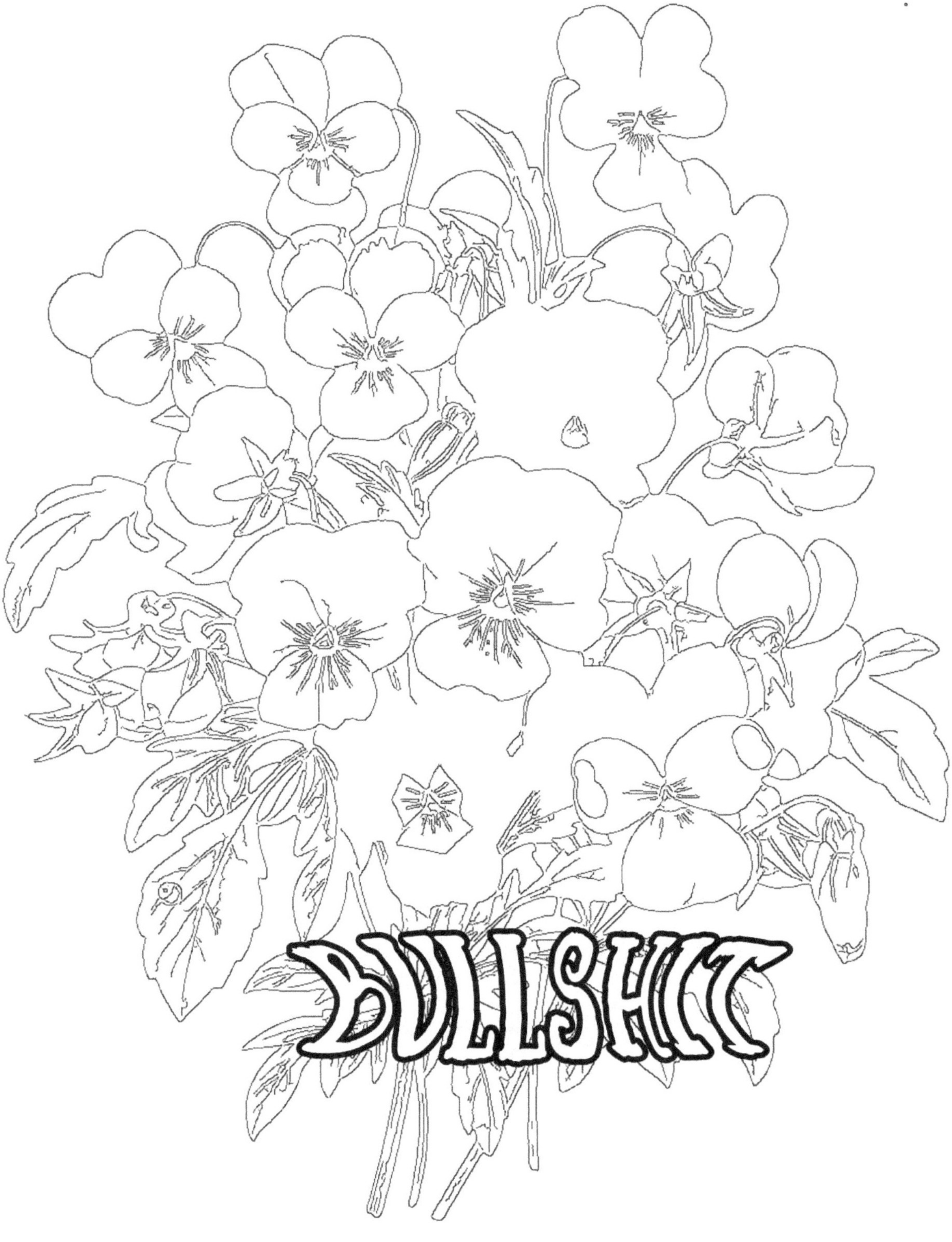
BULLSHIT

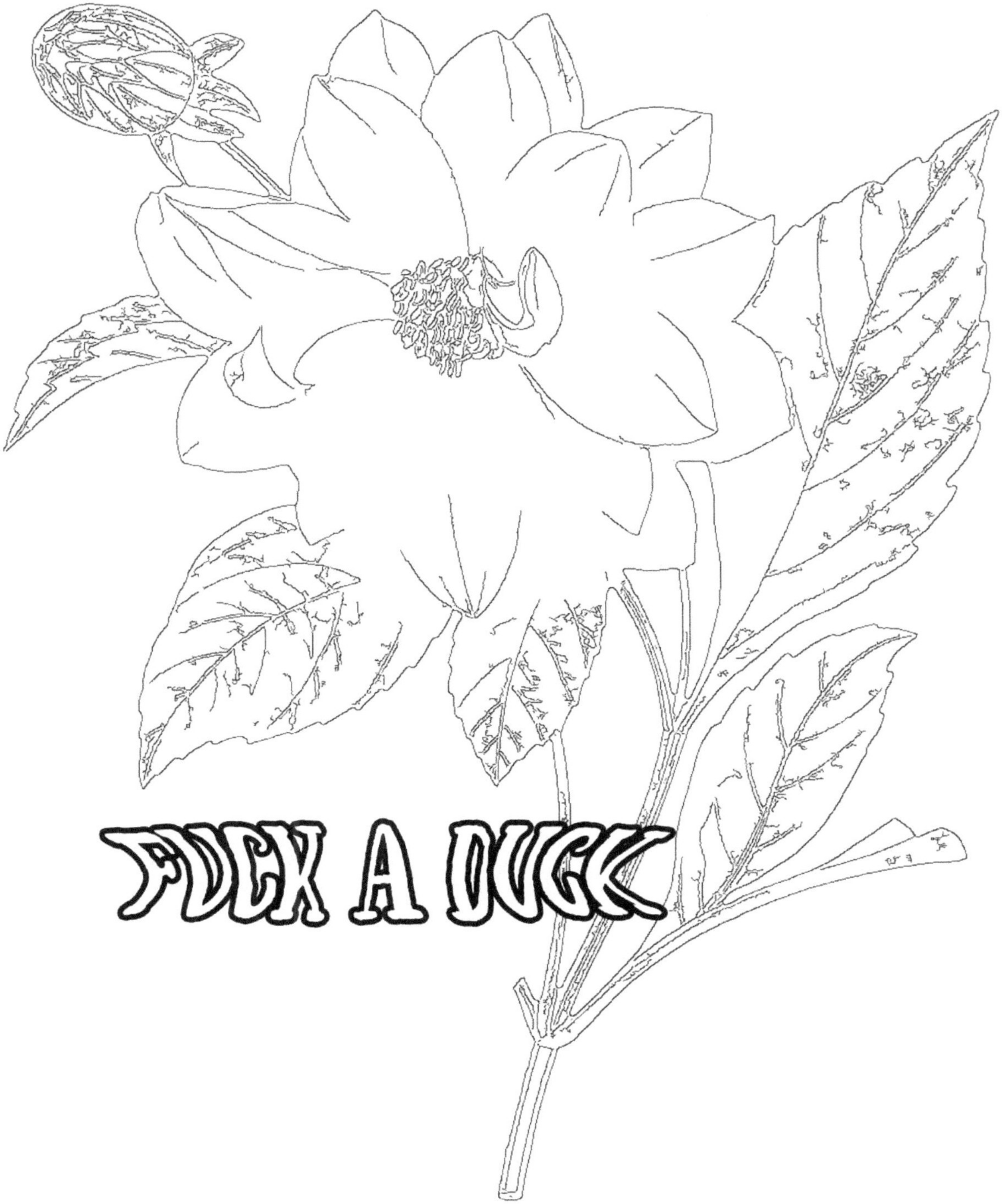
FUCK A DUCK

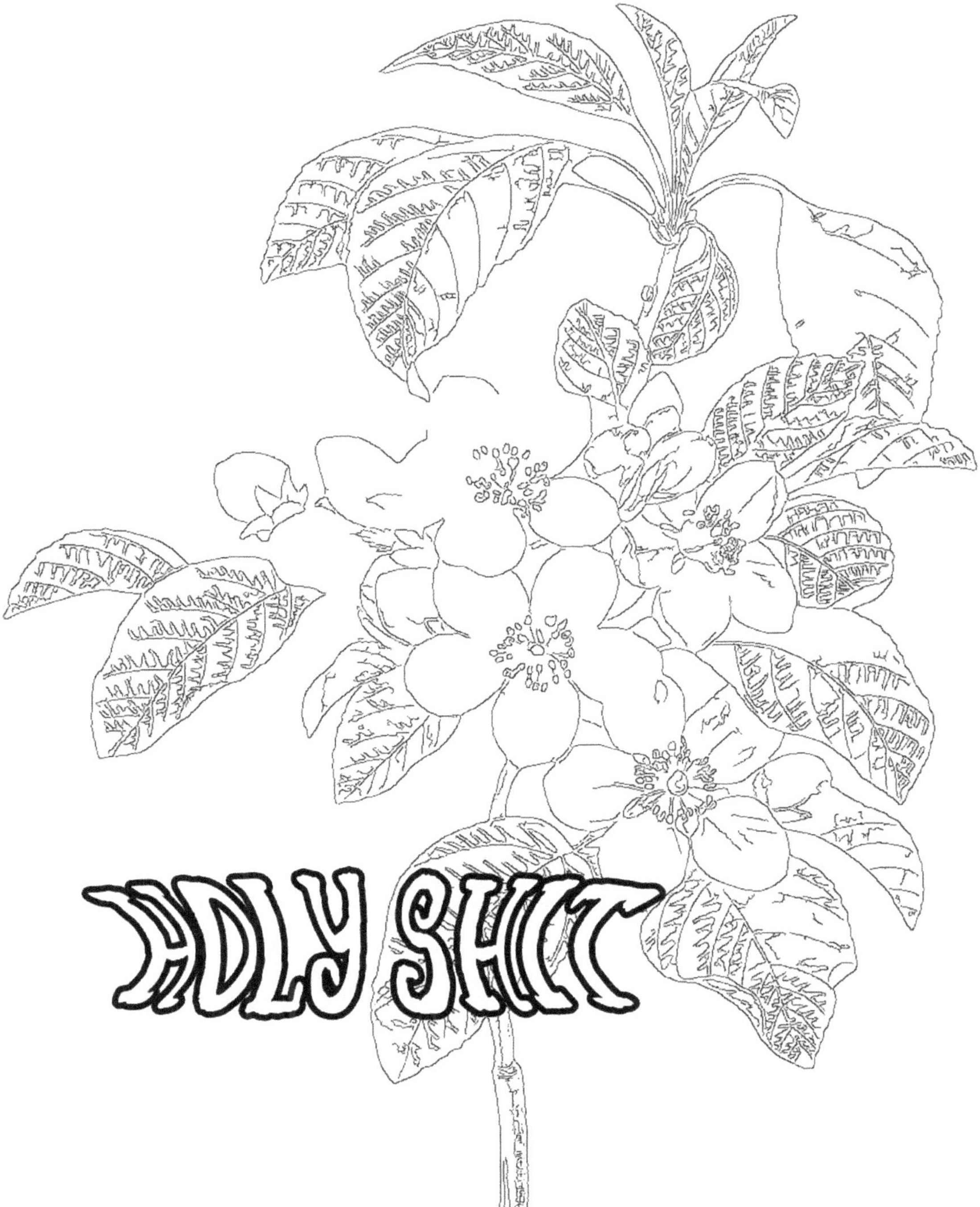
HOLY SHIT

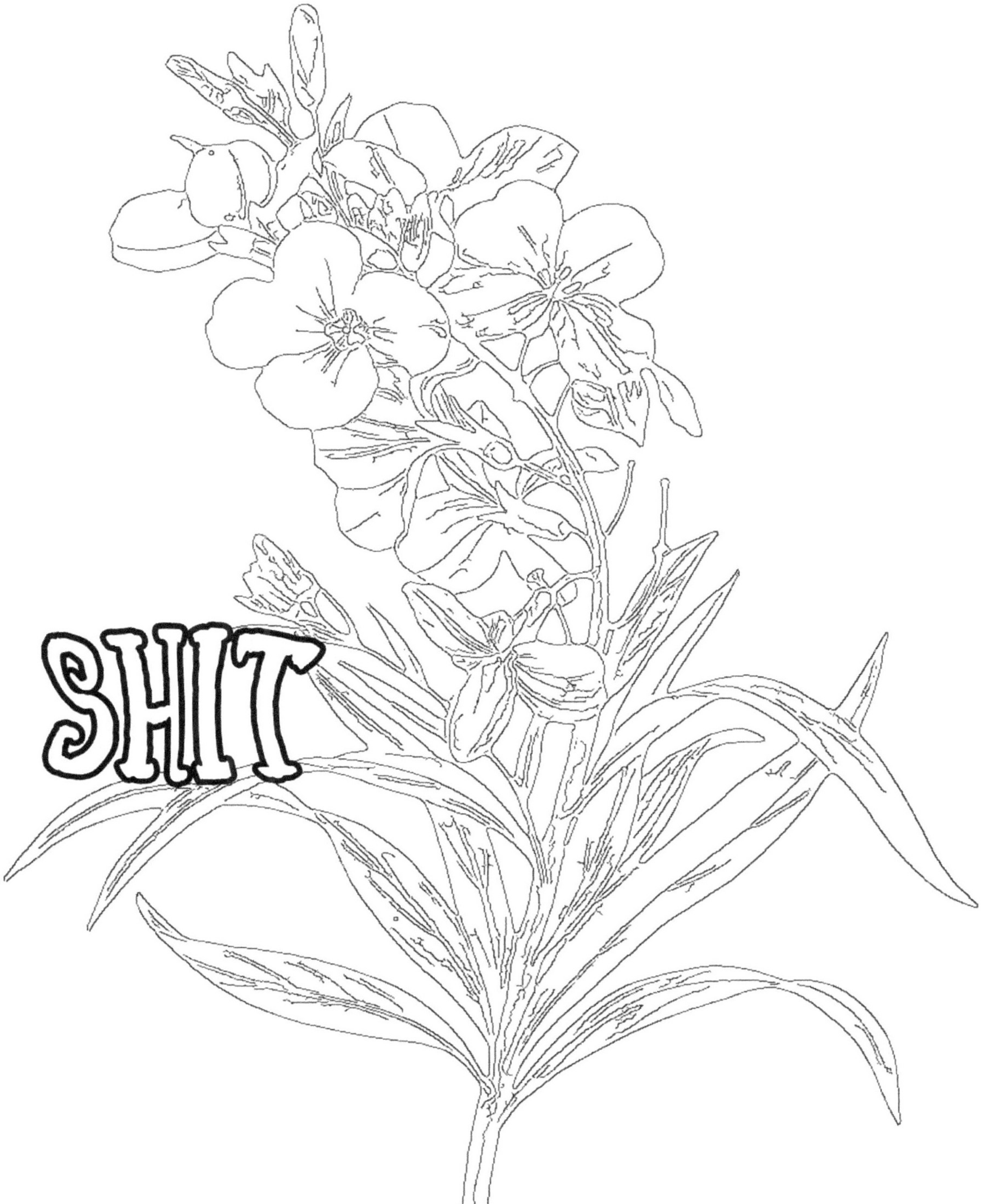
SHIT

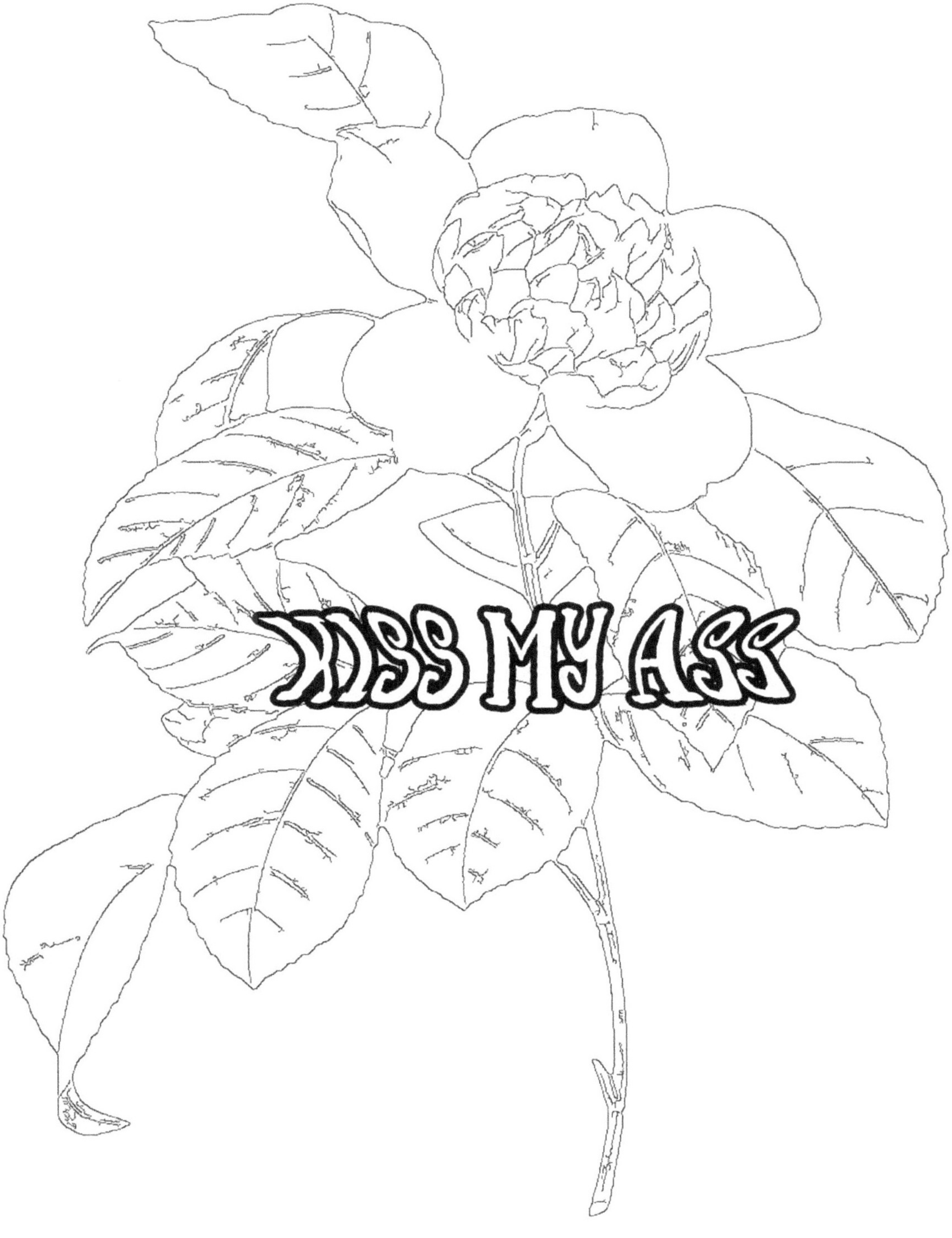
KISS MY ASS

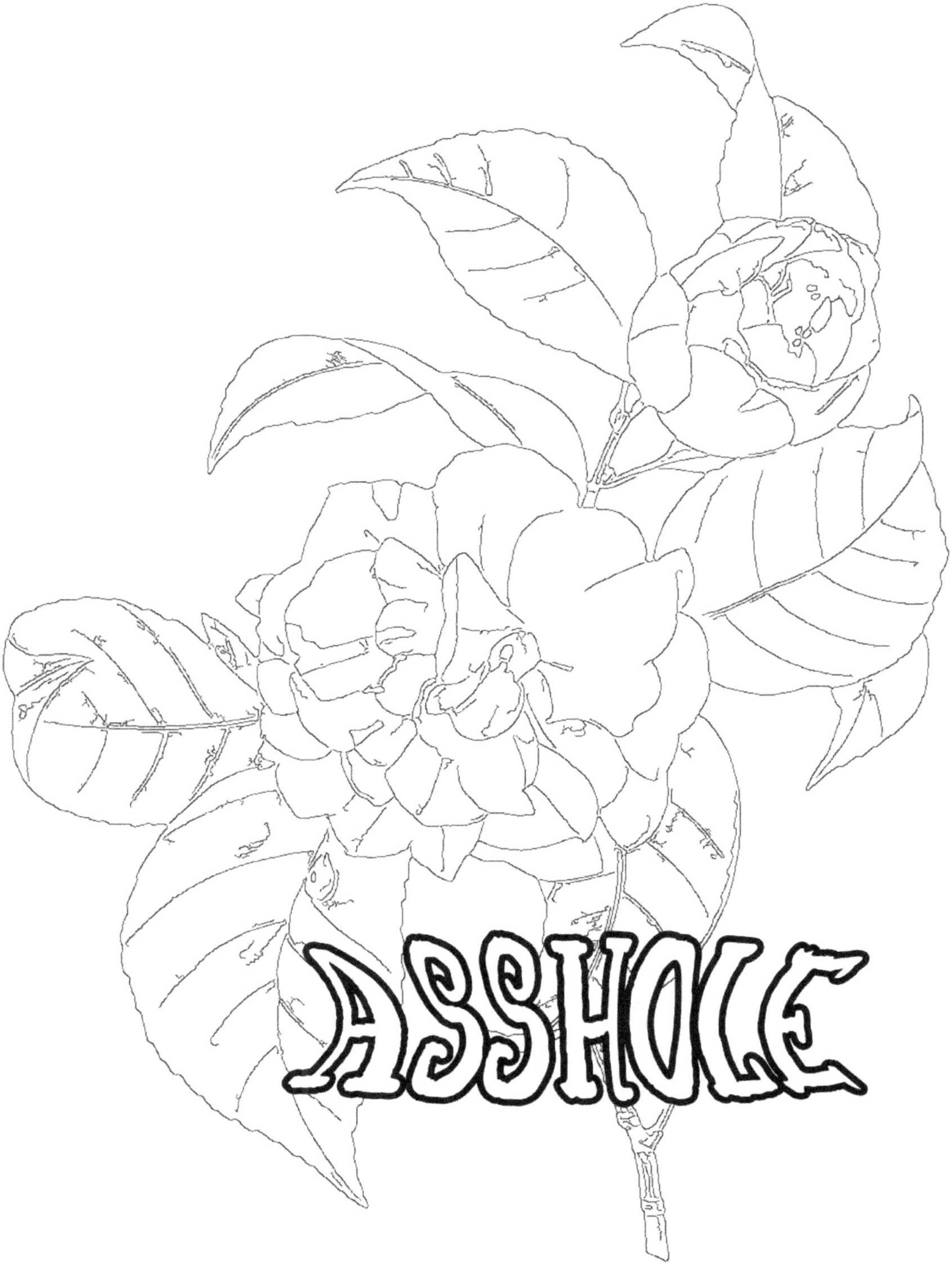
ASSHOLE

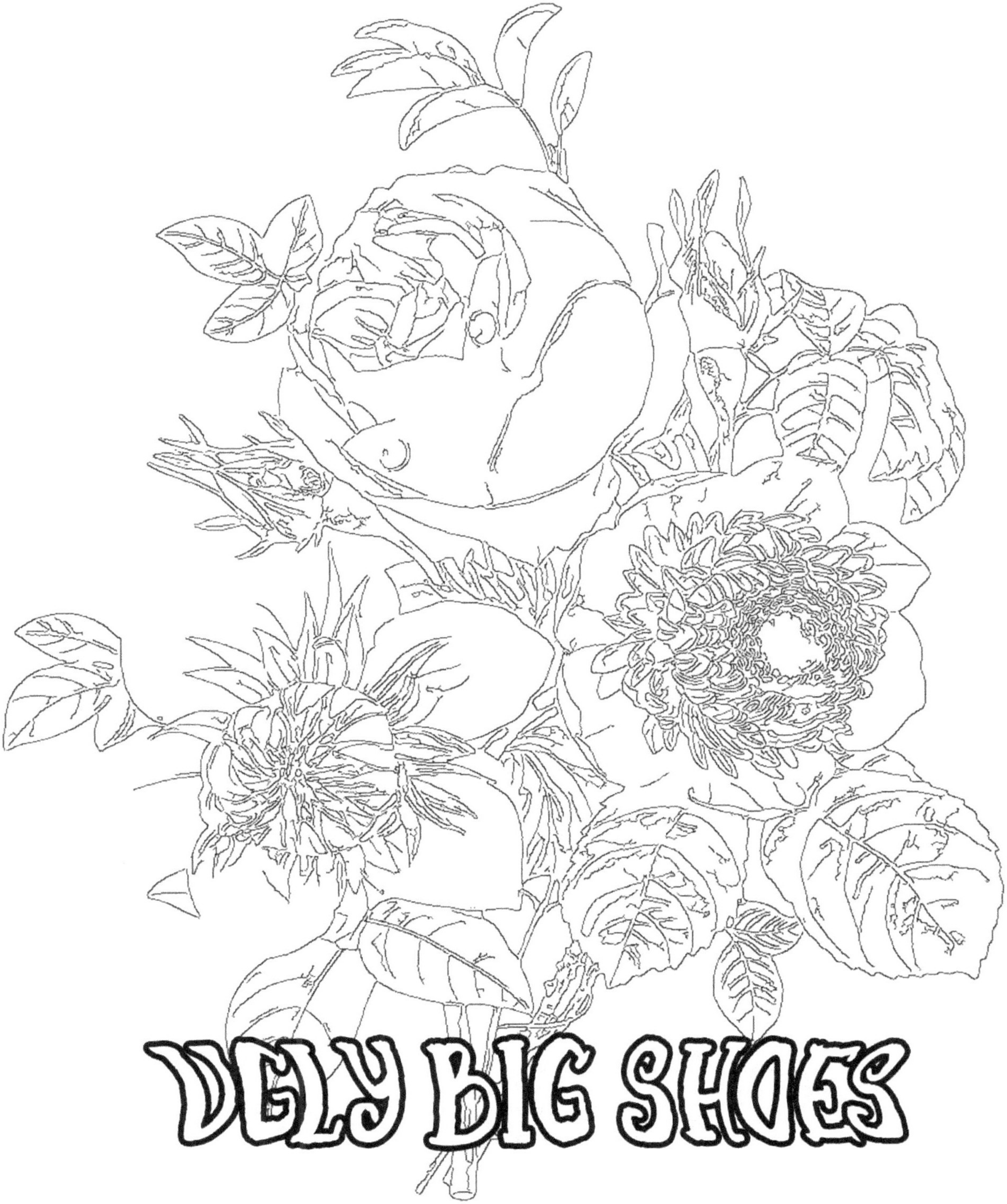
UGLY BIG SHOES

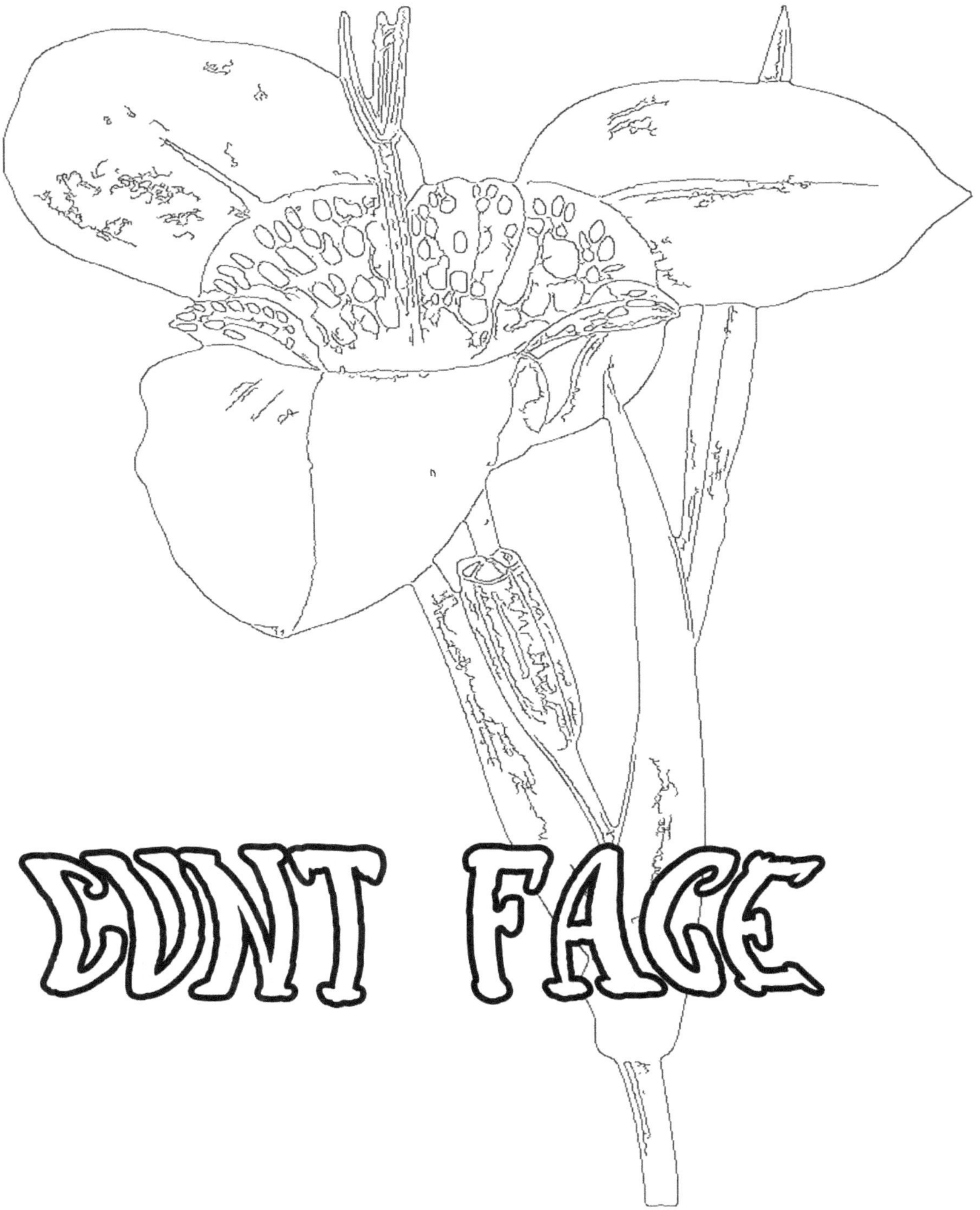
CUNT FACE

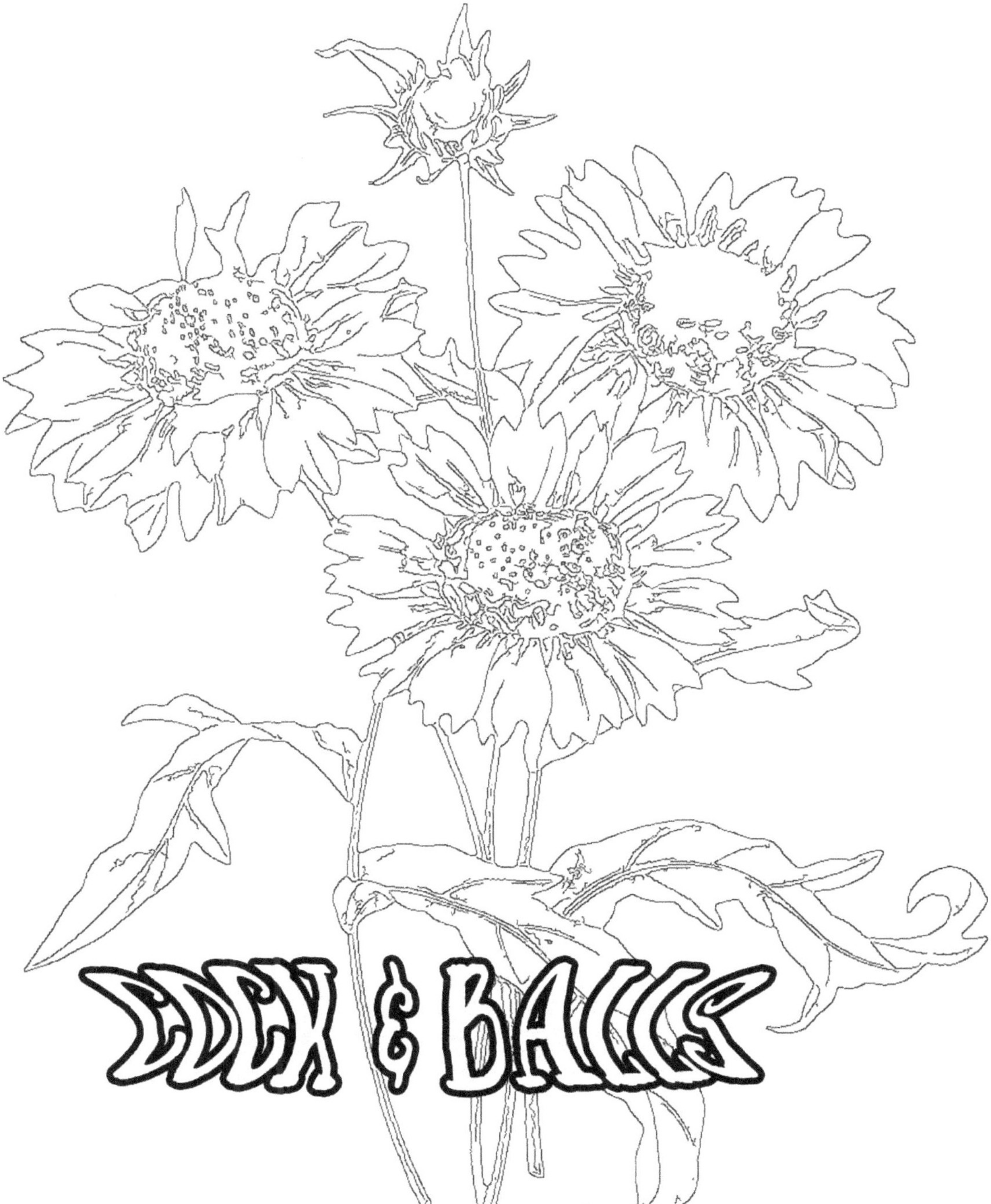
COCK & BALLS

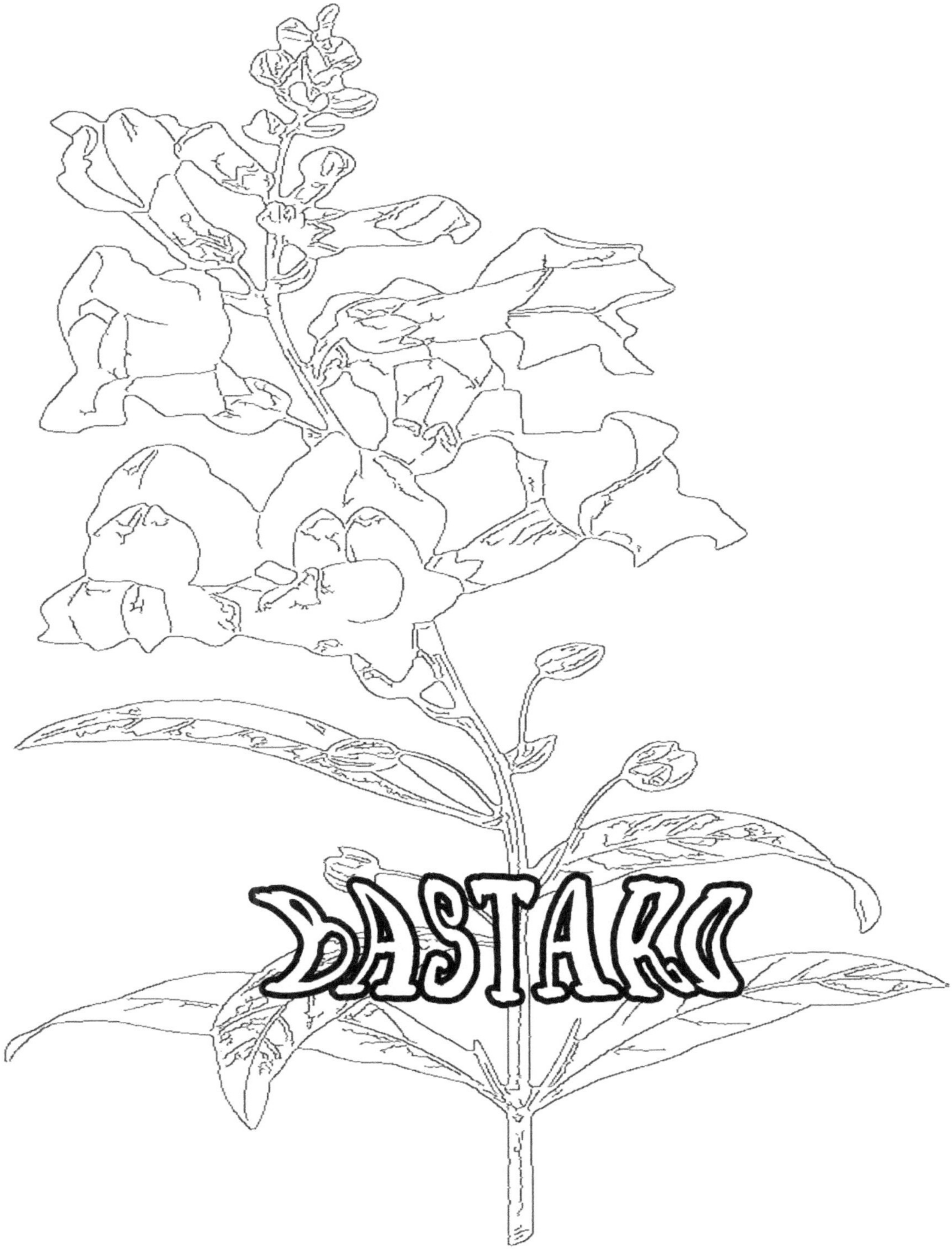
BASTARD

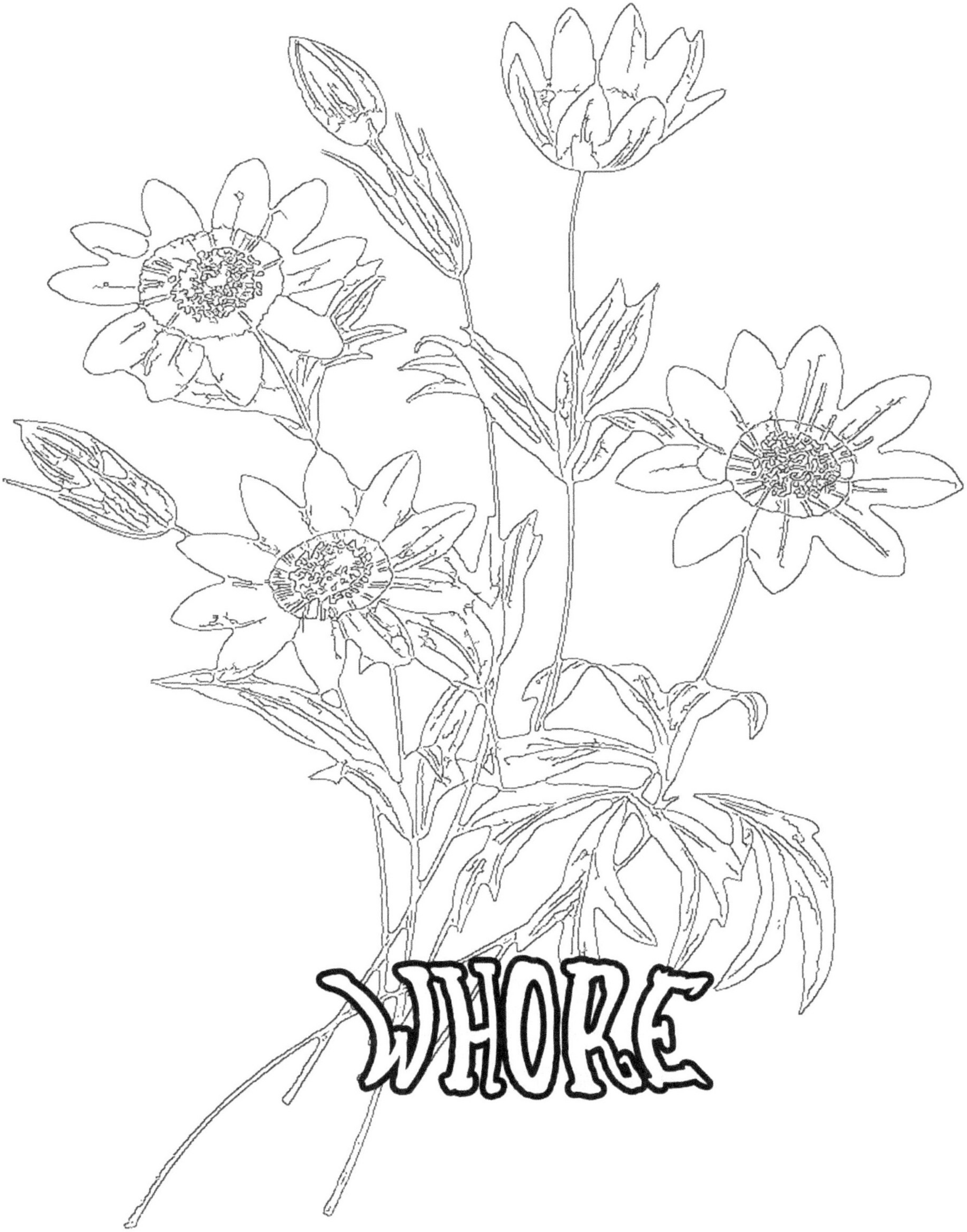
WHORE

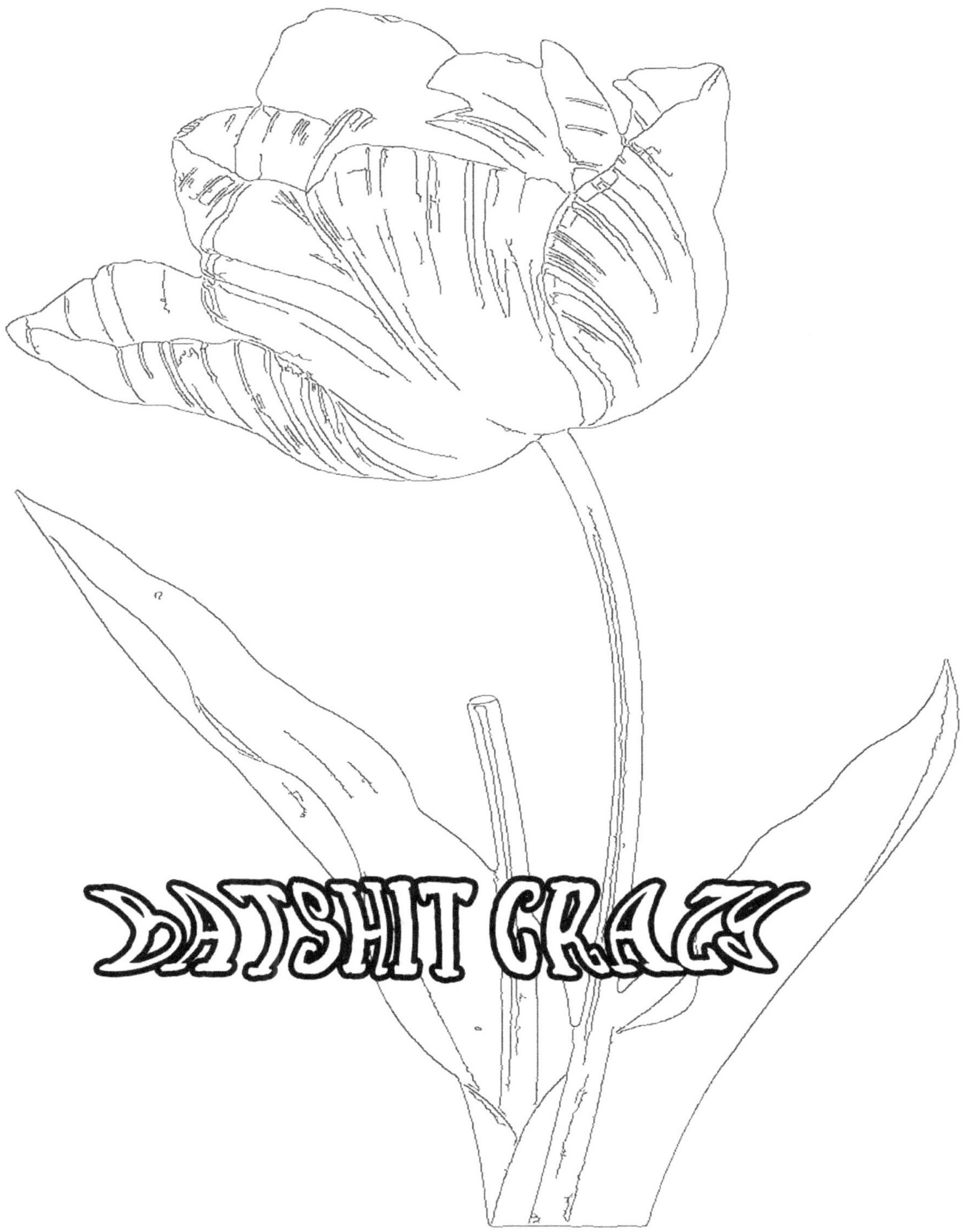
BATSHIT CRAZY

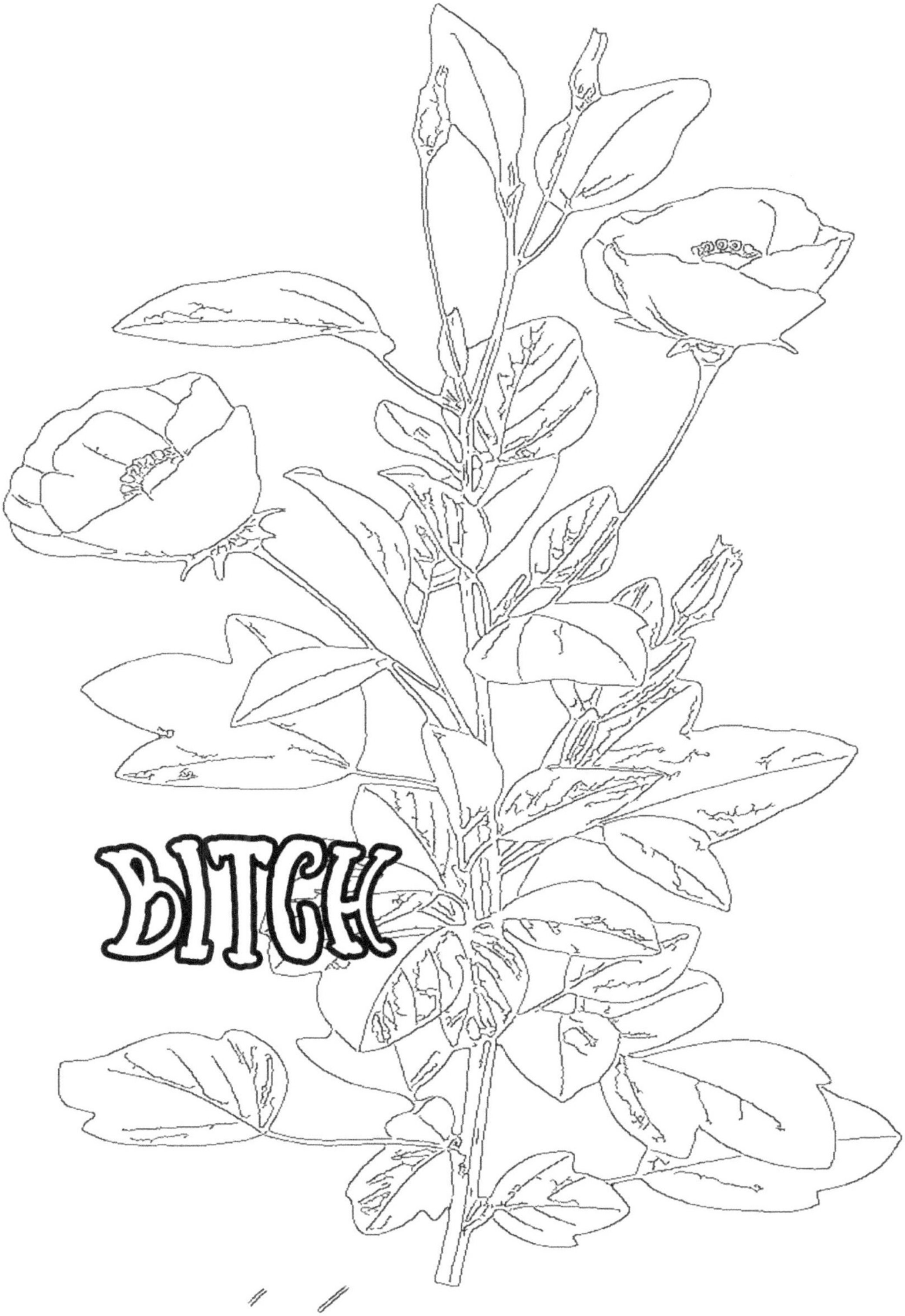
BITCH

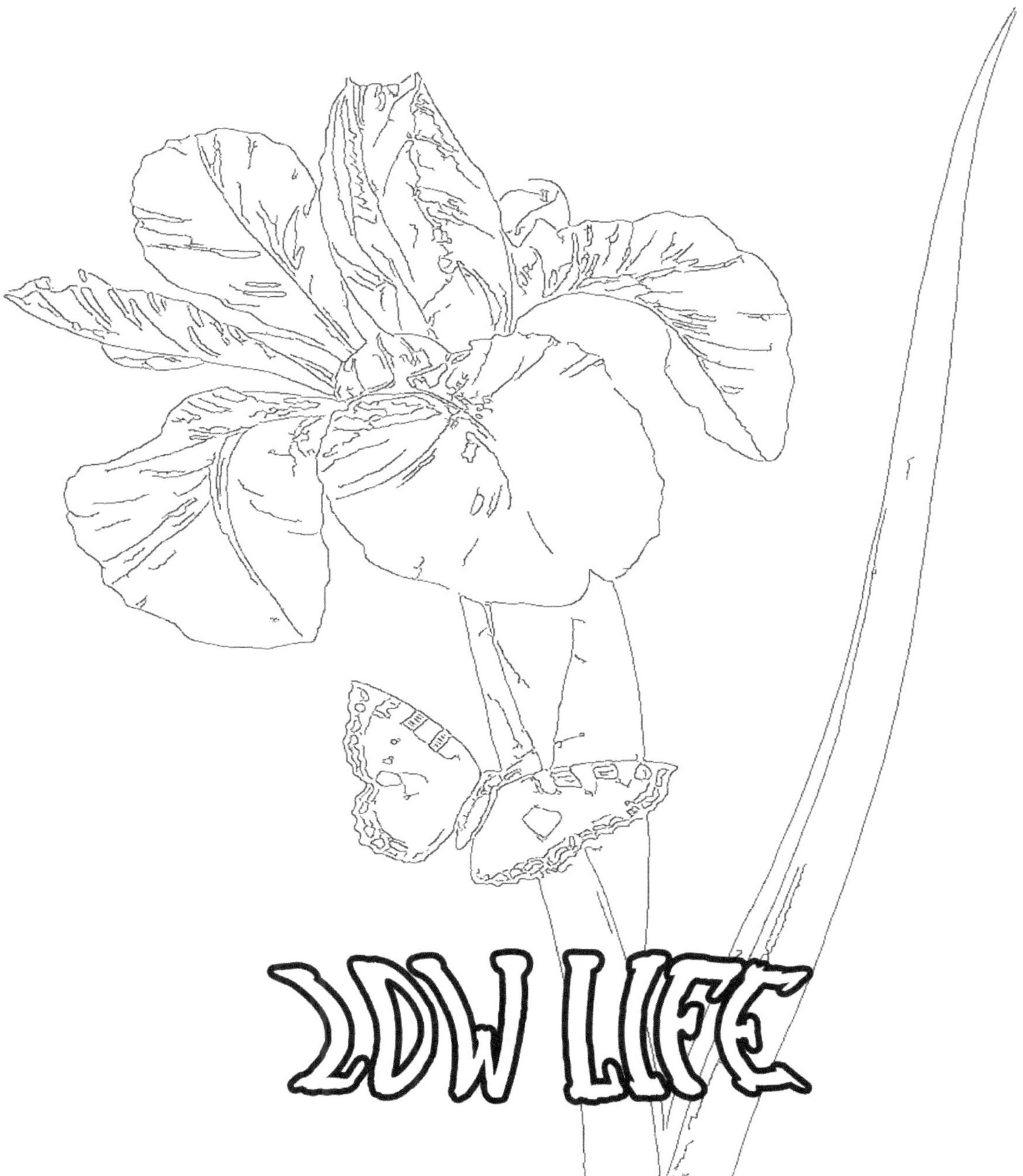
LOW LIFE

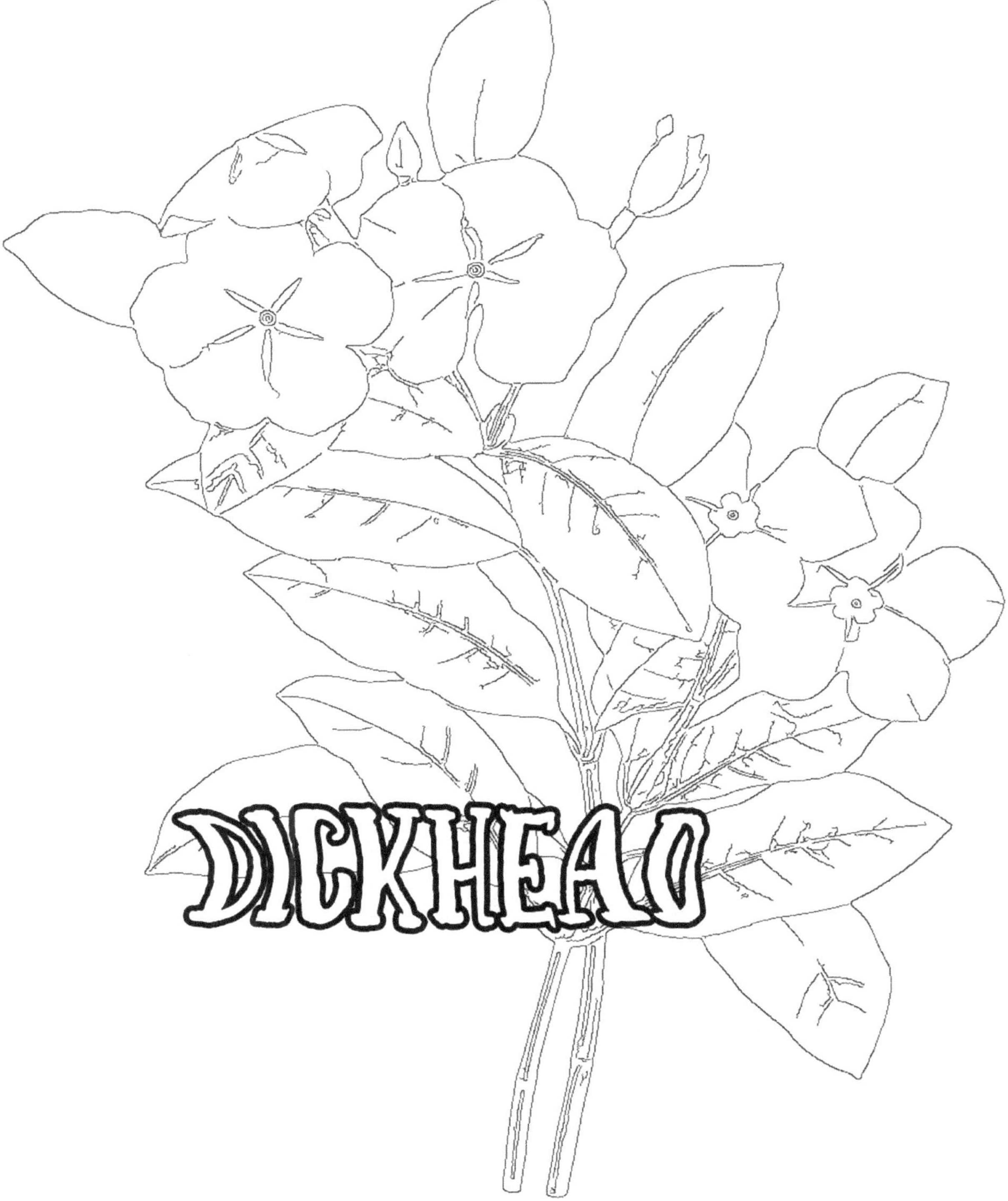
DICKHEAD

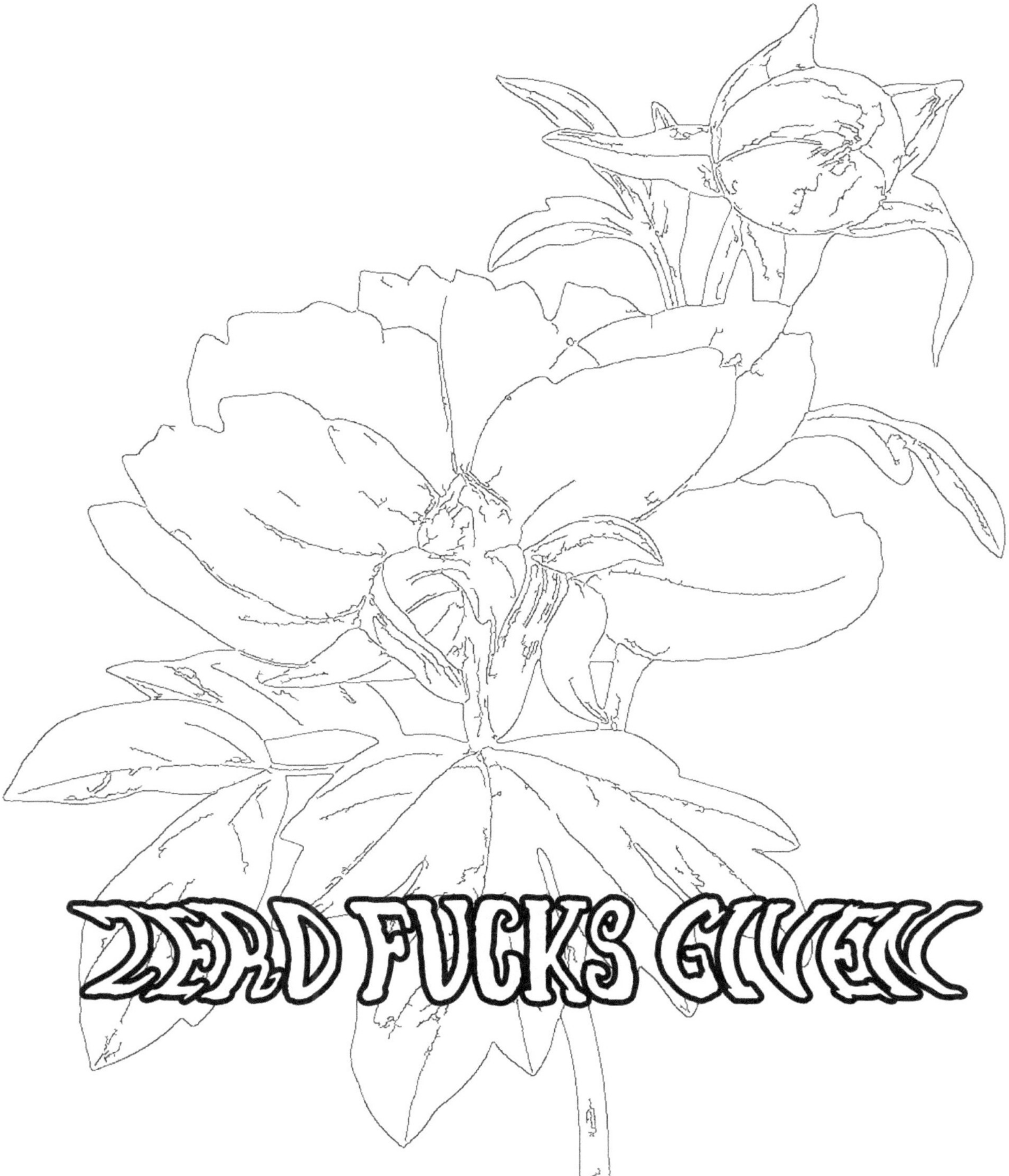
ZERO FUCKS GIVEN

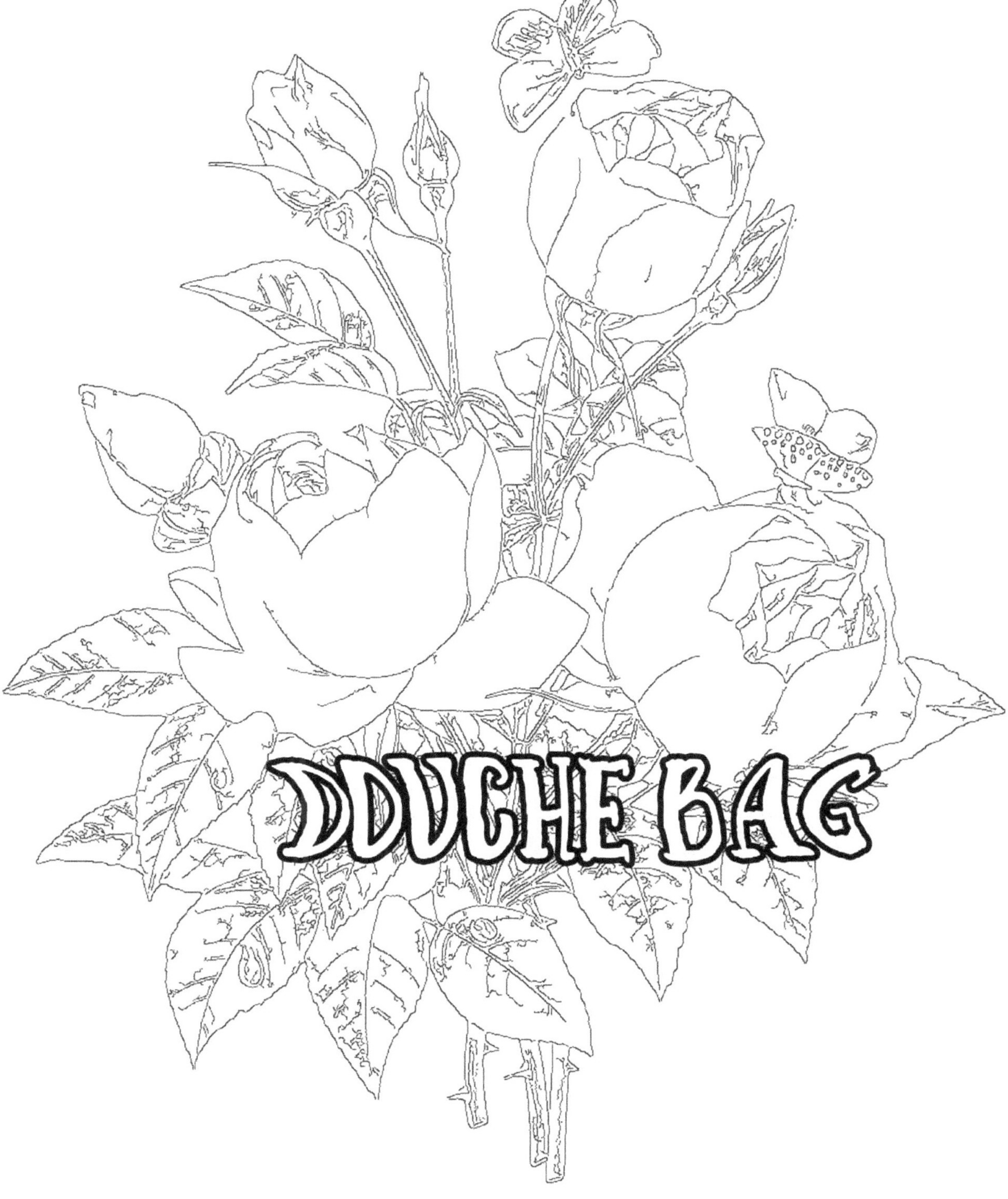
DOUCHE BAG

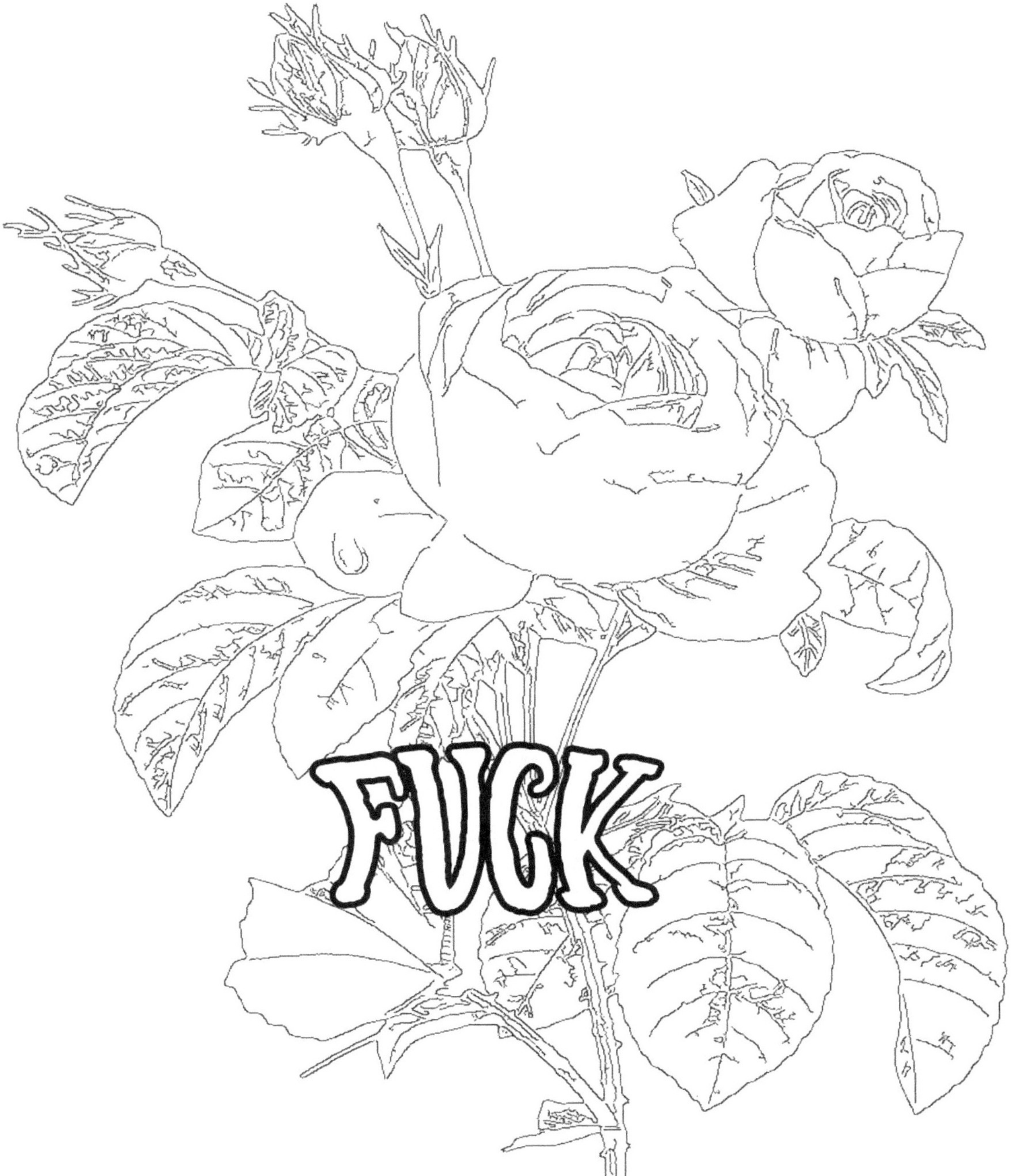
FUCK

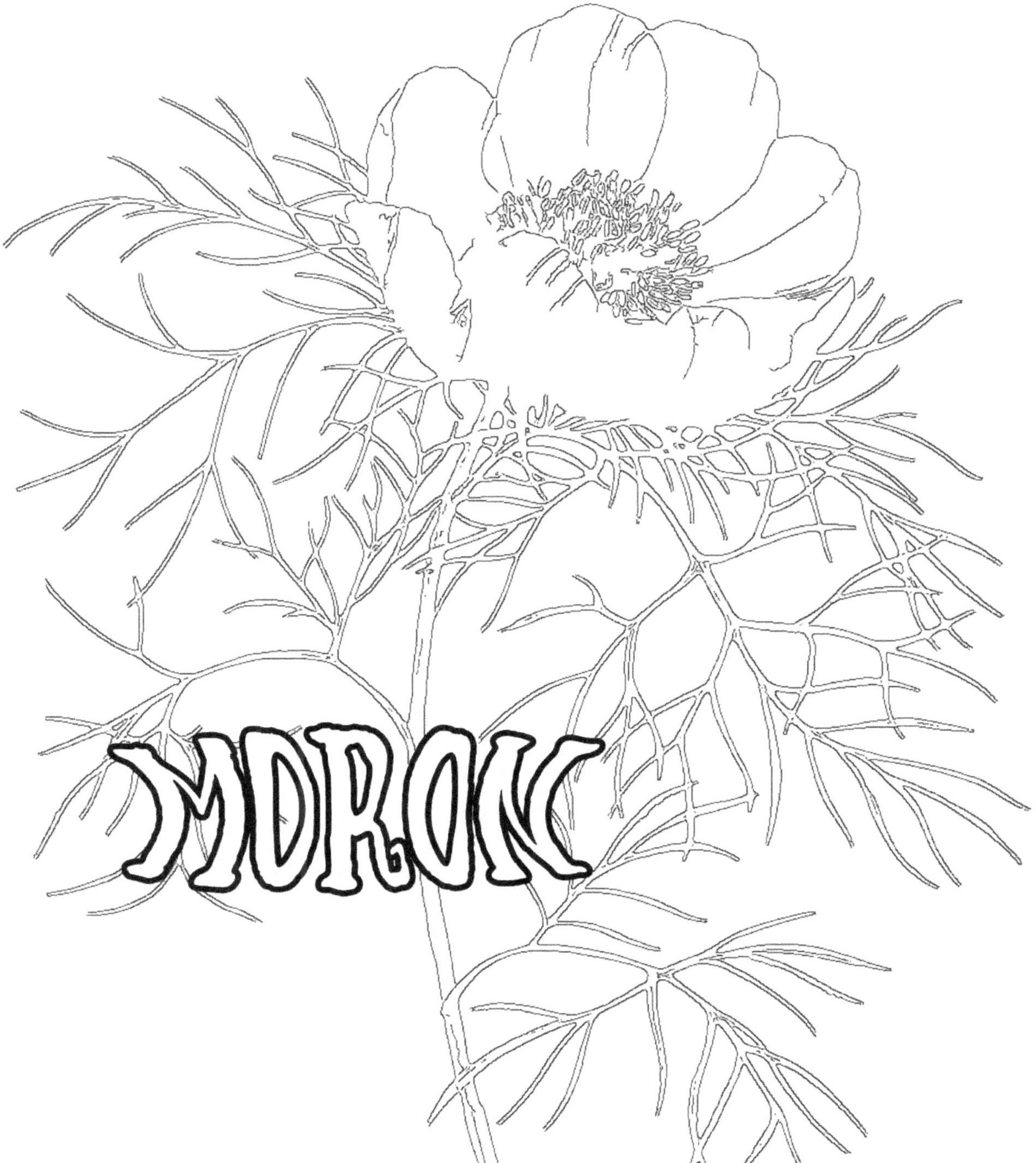
MORON

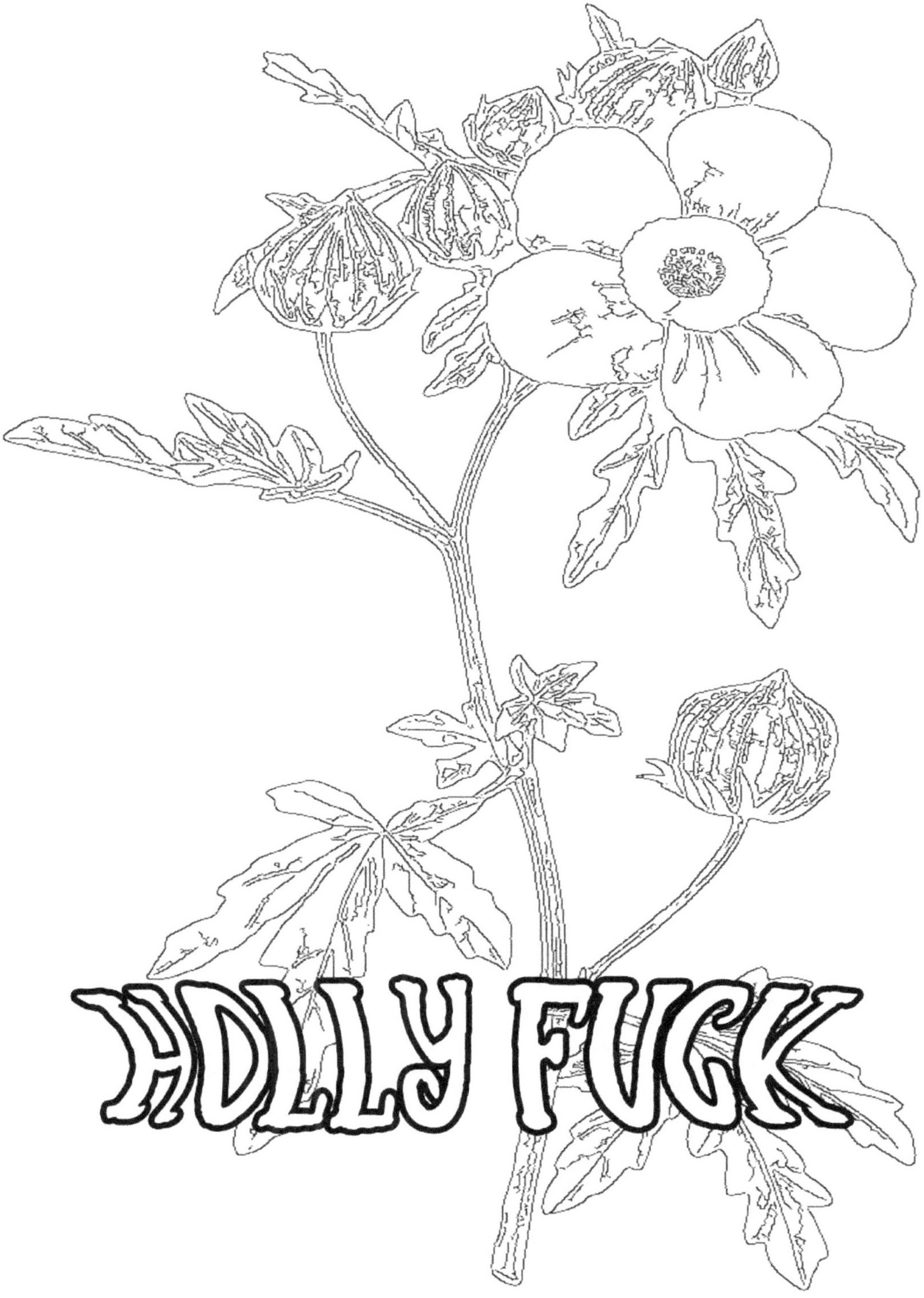
HOLLY FUCK

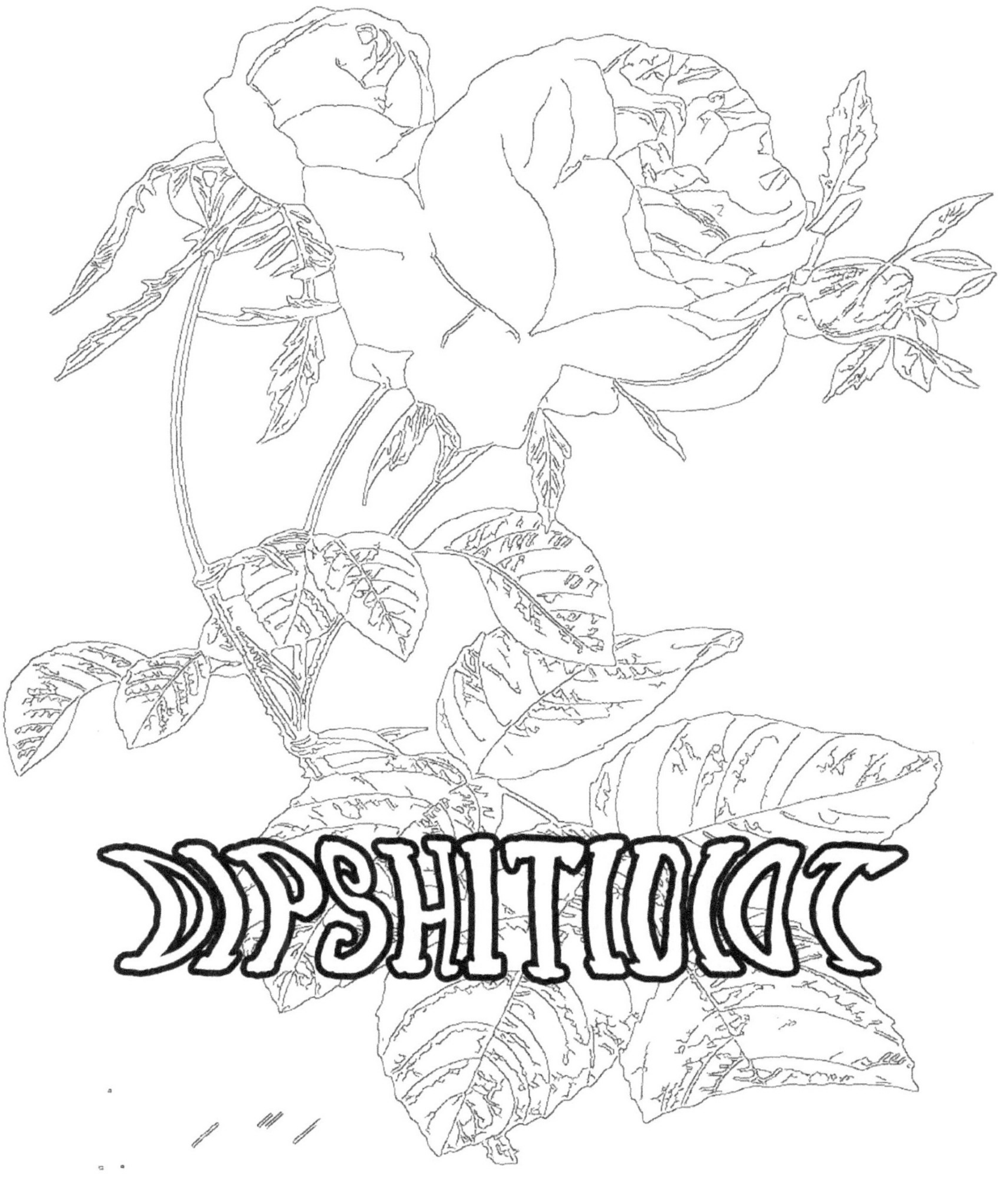
DIPSHITIDIOT

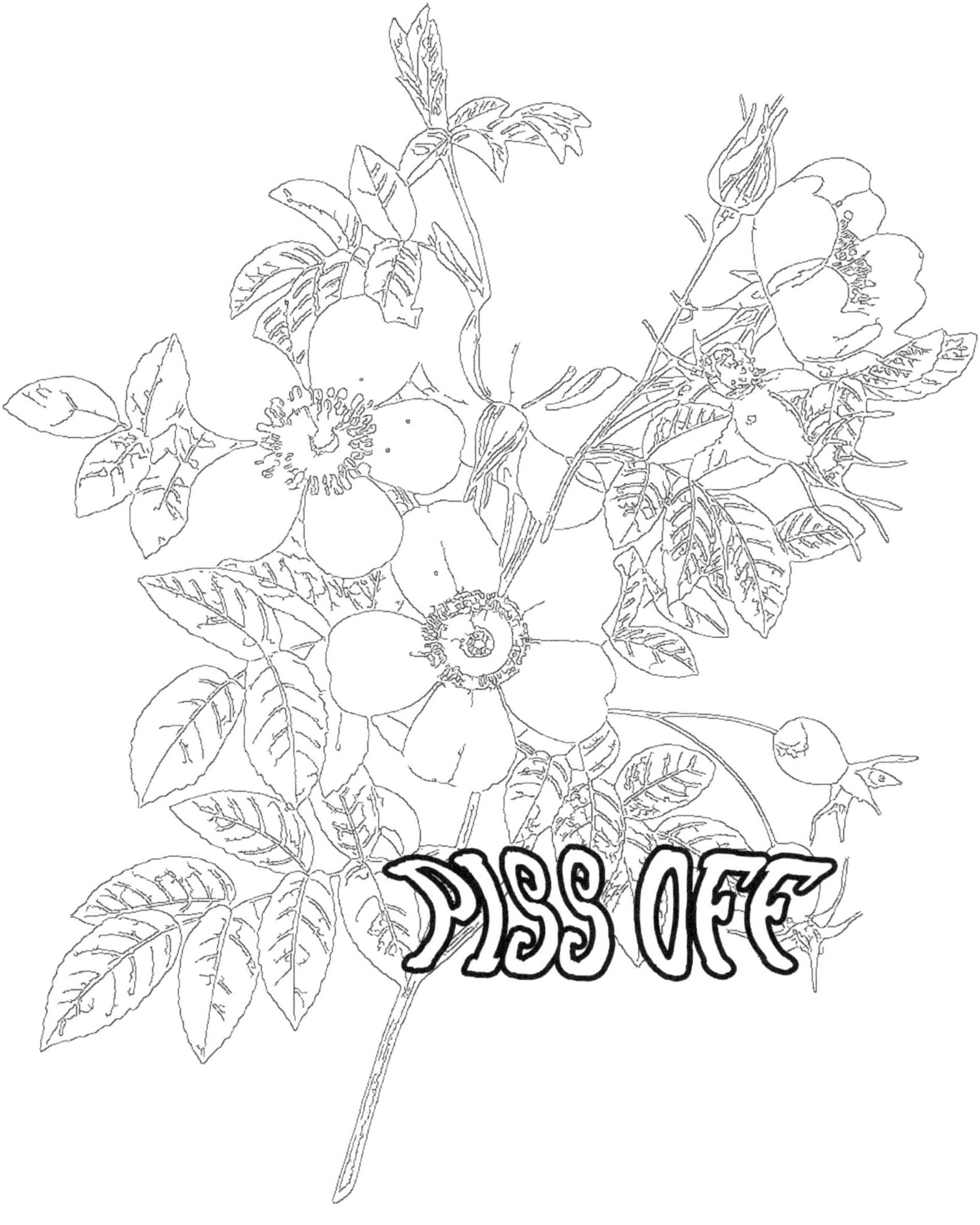
PISS OFF

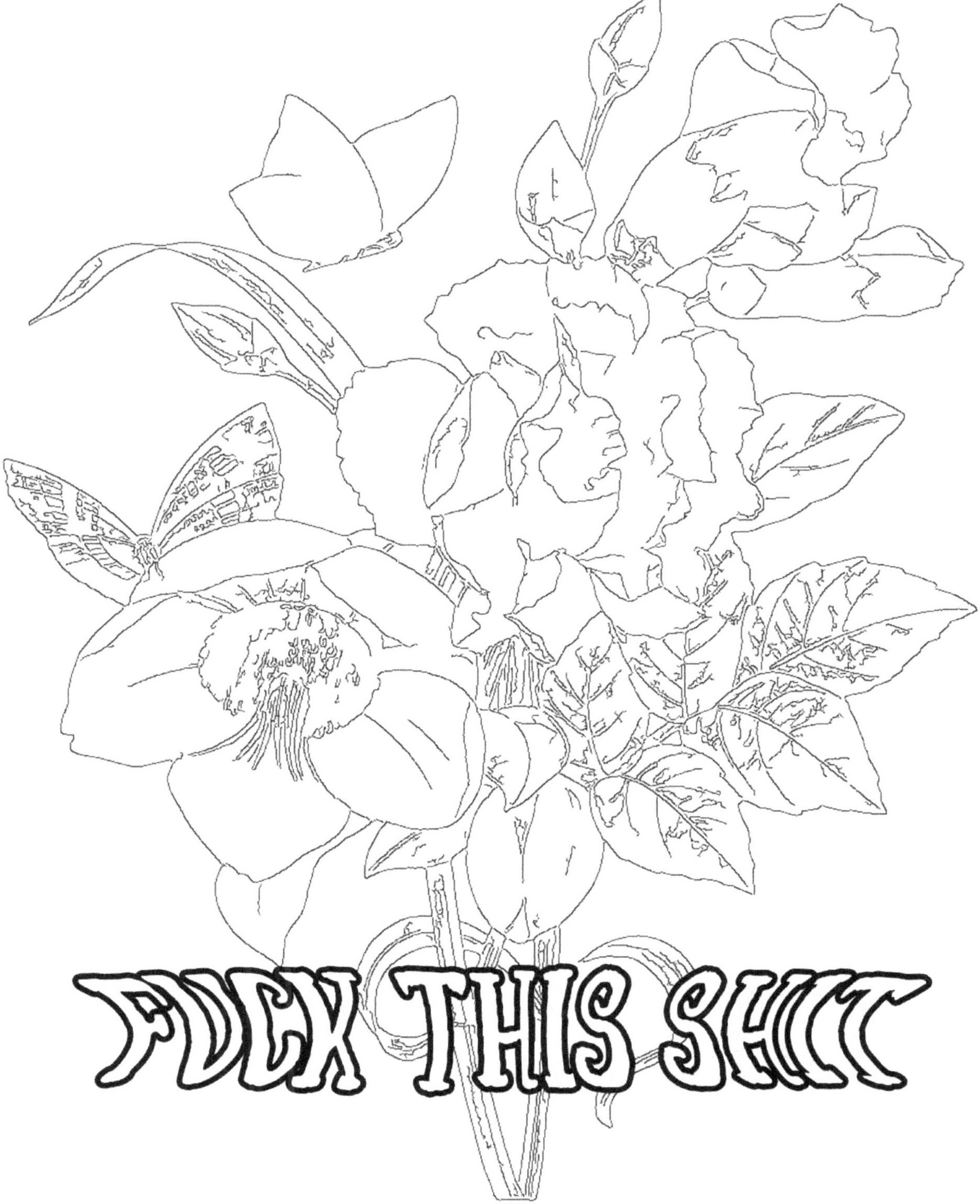
FUCK THIS SHIT

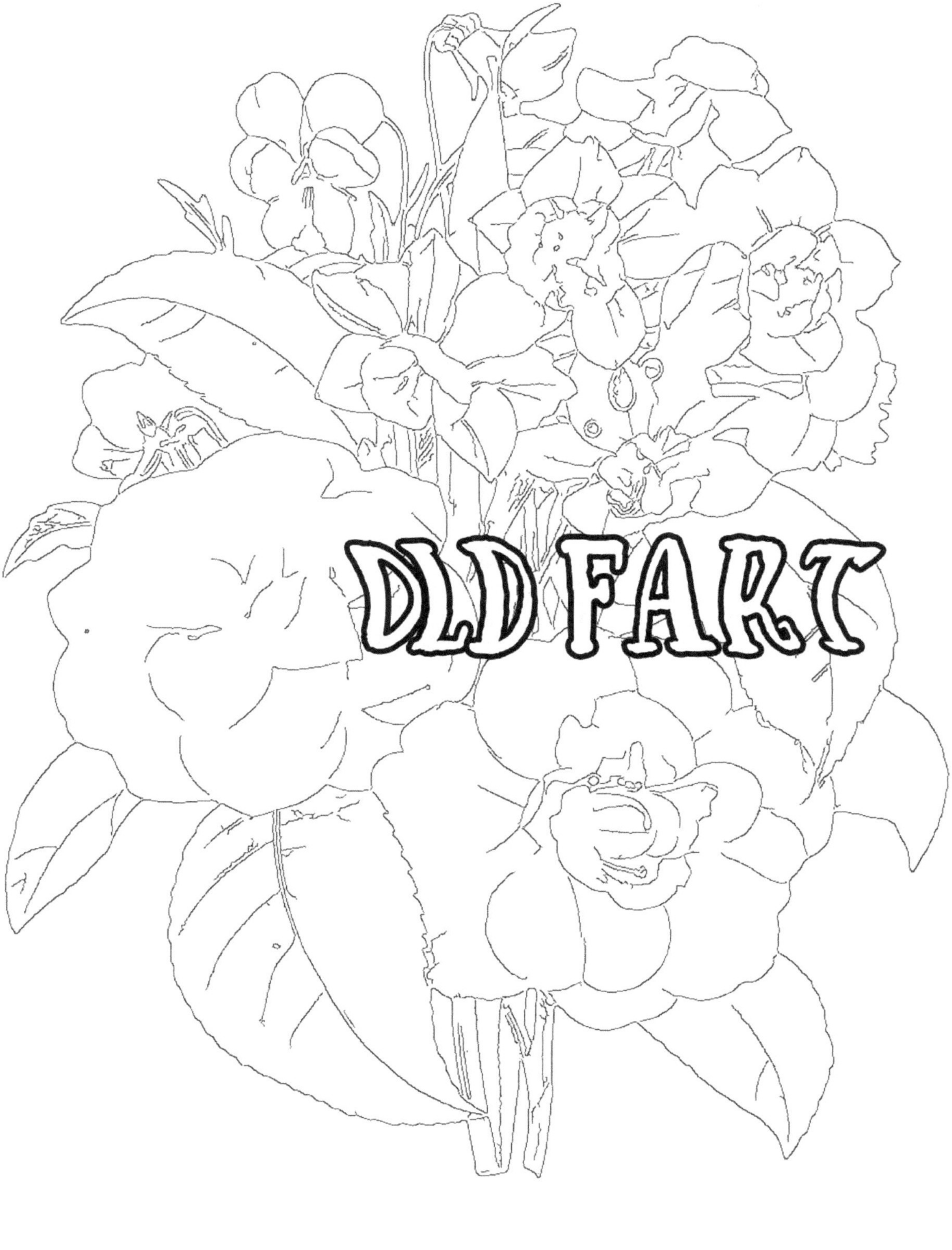
OLD FART

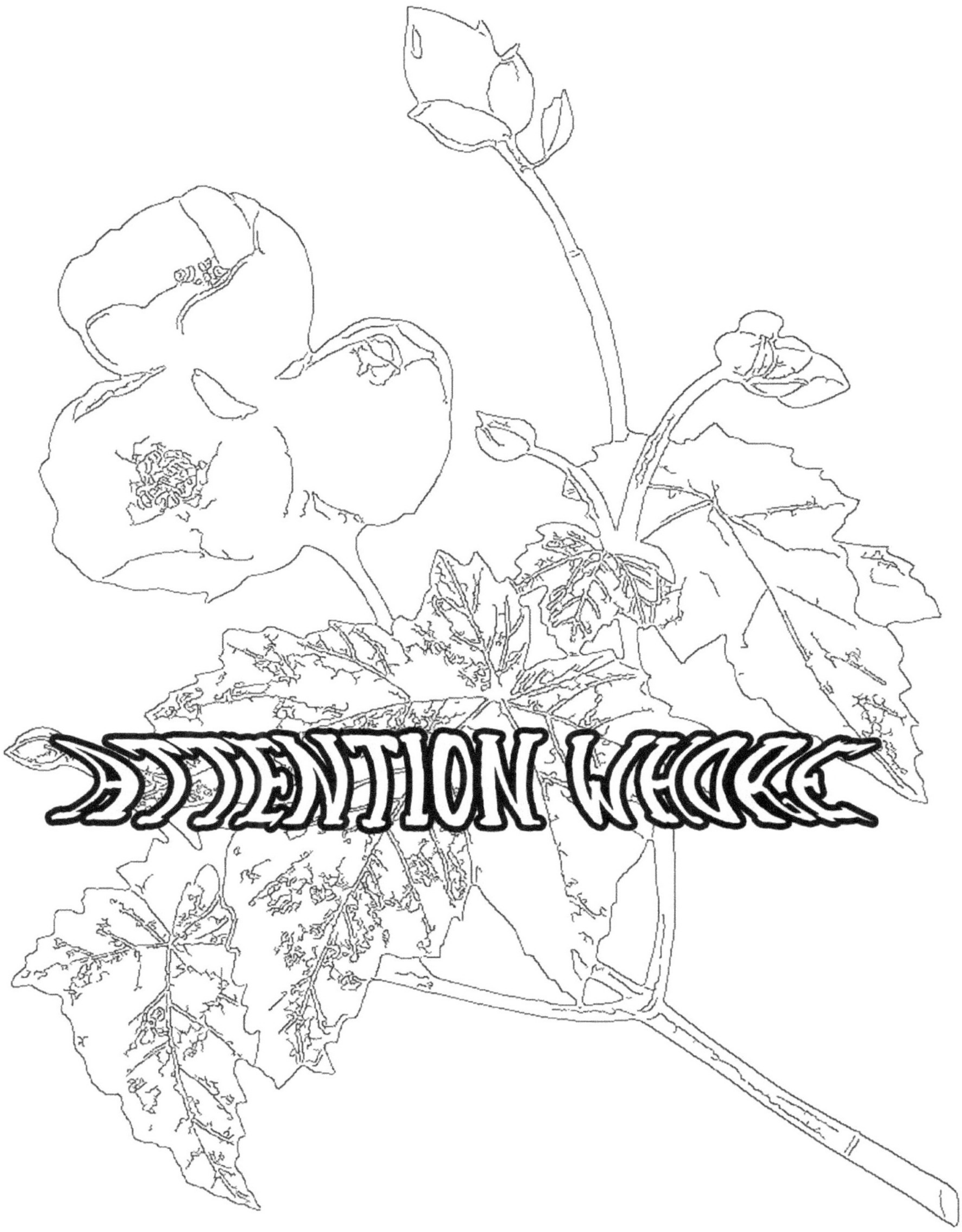
ATTENTION WHORE

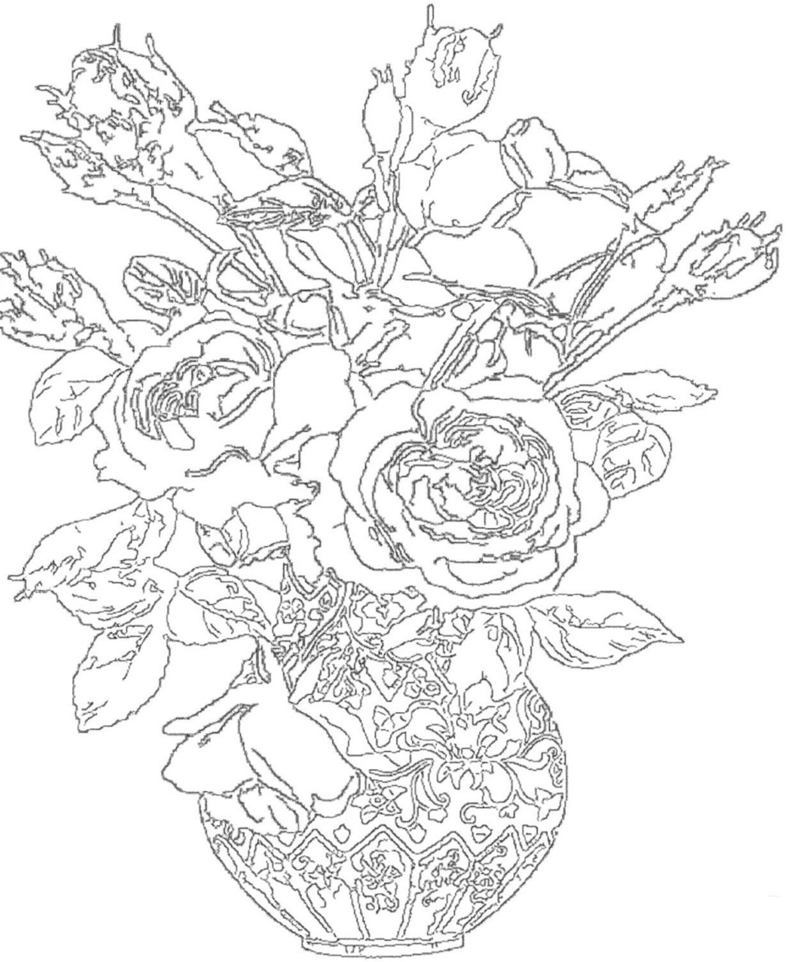

Have a good day.

www.ingramcontent.com/pod-product-compliance
Lightning Source LLC
Chambersburg PA
CBHW081620220526
45468CB00010B/2964
* 9 7 8 1 9 8 3 4 7 1 7 1 1 *